St. Mary
The Pure and Faithful Dove

St. Mary & St. Demiana Convent

Saint Mary
Children's Saints Series
Copyright © 2021 St. Mary & St. Demiana Convent

All rights reserved.

Designed by the St. Mary & St. Demiana Convent
330 Village Drive
Dawsonville, GA 30534

Published by:
St. Mary & St. Moses Abbey Press
101 S Vista Dr., Sandia, TX 78383
stmabbeypress.com

All rights reserved. No part of this book may be reproduced or transmitted in any form or by any means without written permission from the author and publisher.

Illustrated by: Nancy Mikhael Barsoum
Written by: Mary Crocker

Foreword

"You are the light of the world."

Matthew 5:14

As one body in Christ, our Church is united both in heaven and on earth. We, who live here on this beautiful planet, are well known by those who live up there in the paradise of joy ☺ and every day they look out for us and talk to God on our behalf!

So now it's our turn to get to know them! These saints—the Heroes of our Church and our great role models—are waiting to become our very best friends! As we get to know each one of them personally, we will not only gain companions for our everyday lives but also the valuable partners who walk with us along the road that leads to our beloved Lord Jesus Christ.

With the blessing and prayers of our dear father, His Grace Bishop Youssef, it is with great joy that we present the lives of the saints to our children—the future generation of our Church.

May each new story learned be a flame used to light another's candle until the whole world is lit with the light of the glory of God in His saints!

May this be as great a blessing to you as it has been for us, and may the intercessions of St. Mary and the whole choir of angels and saints be with us all!

In all of history, God set one special girl apart.

Mary had a gentle spirit and devoted heart.

Mary served in the temple until one day, the Angel Gabriel appeared with something special to say.

"Hail to you, full of grace, you will bear God's Son!" Mary humbly answered and said, "May God's will be done."

For Mary chose to believe rather than to fear. She knew God would be with her and make her path clear.

Joseph was set to take Mary as his wife making a promise to God that he would care for her for the rest of his life.

Mary glorified God at the wonder of it all,
and rejoiced to receive this very special call.

Elizabeth, her cousin, had wonderful news too! She who was barren for many years would soon have a baby due!

Joseph protected Mary; he was worried and afraid, so he thought to hide Mary. He kept this in his heart and prayed.

At night, an Angel appeared to Joseph in a wonderful dream saying, "Do not worry, God has a holy plan to redeem."

"Hooray, the time came when the Lord Jesus was born in a manger! Angels, shepherds, and Magi rejoiced, though their safety was in danger."

Again, an angel appeared to Joseph saying, "To Egypt, you must go." Joseph and Mary once again obeyed for God's faithfulness they did know."

At the temple, Simeon and Anna recognized the Messiah, only days old. They glorified the Almighty God and told Mary of the great things that would unfold.

Mary held these sayings in her heart throughout many years. She rejoiced in Jesus's wondrous works; her eyes were filled with tears.

Soon the time came when the perfect Lamb offered Himself as a sacrifice. Mary again obeyed God's will, ready to witness her Son open the gates of Paradise.

Mary's obedience was perfect, all honor and glory is due. It brought us our Lord Jesus, who saved me and you.

Jesus loved his mother so dearly, on the Cross as He hung there,
He told John the Beloved to take her into his care.

Many years later, Jesus came with angels to invite her to her eternal place.

She is now on her throne as Queen of Heaven, where she intercedes for us with grace.

Mary's pure heart points us to her beloved Son until this very day. She is quick to hear our prayers and to help us in every way.

Her example of courage, faith, and purity shine eternally for all to see. The most blessed among all women, the beautiful dove, and Moses' burning tree.

www.ingramcontent.com/pod-product-compliance
Lightning Source LLC
Chambersburg PA
CBHW041809040426
42449CB00001B/35